*The Intellectual Appeal of Catholicism
and the Idea of a Catholic University*

The Intellectual

Appeal of

Catholicism

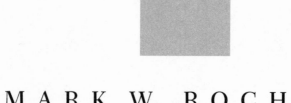

M A R K   W.   R O C H E

& the

Idea of a

Catholic

University

Foreword by Theodore M. Hesburgh, C.S.C.

UNIVERSITY OF NOTRE DAME PRESS

Notre Dame, Indiana

Manufactured in the United States of America

Reprinted in 2008

Library of Congress Cataloging-in-Publication Data
Roche, Mark W.
  The intellectual appeal of Catholicism and the idea
of a Catholic university / Mark W. Roche ; foreword by
Theodore M. Hesburgh.
    p.   cm.
  Includes bibliographical references.
  ISBN 13: 978-0-268-01196-3 (pbk. : alk. paper)
  ISBN 10: 0-268-01196-6 (pbk. : alk. paper)
  1. Catholic universities and colleges—Philosophy.
2. Catholic Church—Education—United States.
3. Catholic Church—Doctrines.   I. Title.
LC487.R59   2003
378'.0712—dc21

                                        2003007213

∞ *This book is printed on acid-free paper.*

Contents

Foreword

I have always been deeply concerned about the ideal and reality of Notre Dame as a great Catholic university. A few years ago this idea was becoming a reason for a kind of intellectual warfare among the faculty. At that time I published a volume called *The Challenge and Promise of a Catholic University* in which about thirty of us set forth our ideas on the subject. The great value of this publication was that the internecine warfare almost immediately ceased because the main protagonists of this or that point of view had a chance to say how they saw it. And that was that.

However, the notion of a Catholic university is still a matter of intellectual debate. Recently, Mark Roche, Dean of Notre Dame's College of Arts and Letters, sent me a copy of an article he had prepared on the intellectual appeal of Catholicism and the idea of a Catholic university. This became a chapter in a volume of conference proceedings called *The Future of Religious Colleges*, but Mark wisely kept the copyright to himself.

I was very much impressed by the article, which I think presents the case as well as I had seen it presented intellectually over many years. It occurred to me that it would be a shame to have so good an article rest among a number of others in a book that could easily be overlooked. Anyway, I proposed to Mark that, since he had the copyright, we might reproduce his chapter as a monograph that could receive wide distribution and attention.

Mark presents a clear, precise, and idealistic view of a Catholic university. His arguments will appeal to those interested in the distinctive character of a Catholic university—students and faculty, parents and graduates, donors and friends, administrators and trustees. The original essay was focused on Notre Dame, but the revision offers a more general view of the challenge and promise of a Catholic university. The essay creates a better understanding of what a Catholic university is here at home, but all the outstanding members of the International Federation of Catholic Universities around the world, not only those in the United States, will recognize its importance.

I believe we need more and more of this kind of presentation to give us a sense of our own identity, which I think gets pretty blurred at times. In some instances the Catholic identity is taken for granted, and in others it is barely understood. In a short amount of space Mark makes visible the ideal of a Catholic university. I think he has done a stellar task of presenting the case, as intellectually valid as I have ever seen one. Even Cardinal Newman did not do as well in his classic *The Idea of a University*.

One of the things that I especially like in Mark's essay is the prominence he gives to the Holy Spirit, which is too often neglected in our thinking. If a Catholic university is to fulfill its mission, it must be intimate with the light, the inspiration, and the courage that the Holy Spirit brings. The intangible presence of God in our lives brings us closer to truth and to one another. A Catholic university and a Catholic community are animated by the breath of the Holy Spirit, which brings wisdom and courage as we face challenges and difficulties.

Mark is involved in the active work of helping to build a great Catholic university. His work is replete with vision and dreams for the future. He has wonderful insight into where we should be, and what needs to be done to get there. It is not by chance that in leading the College of Arts and Letters, he would be led to think deeply and passionately about these higher questions. Being at a special and prayerful place like Notre Dame doesn't hurt, either.

Mark's essay is very ecumenical in its outreach to scholars who are not Catholic. It shows how a Catholic university can make a difference, how it can be a great university and still be something more. This trenchant and intellectual presentation gives us hope that by exploring the ultimate questions and ultimate values that distinguish a great Catholic university, we may come ever closer to realizing the living unity of knowledge and dignity, wisdom and grace, God and truth.

Theodore M. Hesburgh, C.S.C.
President Emeritus
University of Notre Dame

The Intellectual Appeal of Catholicism and the Idea of a Catholic University

Mark W. Roche

The idea of "a Catholic university" is "a contradiction in terms," quipped George Bernard Shaw exactly one century ago (247). Might it not be wiser to consider the idea a tautology? The words "Catholic" and "university" have the same root meaning. Historically, a connection exists as well: the first universities were founded in Catholic Europe. In addition, the Catholic tradition shares much in common with the ideals of a university. Supporting Shaw's witticism, however, a modern cliché suggests that educated persons and intellectuals cannot be religious or, if they are religious, that they cannot take their religion very seriously. Certainly, this widespread attitude, which Stephen Carter has outlined in *The Culture of Disbelief*, has been one of the factors contributing to modern skepticism concerning the idea of a religious university of any kind. Because the idea of a Catholic university seems so anomalous to contemporary consciousness, even some of its greatest supporters feel embarrassed when articulating the idea of Catholic character to a skeptical academic audience. In such a climate, those who support the idea of building a great Catholic university need to work harder at finding a vocabulary that articulates the distinct mission of a Catholic university in such a way as to be both true to the Catholic tradition and inviting to nonreligious intellectuals, whether at Catholic or at secular universities.[1]

As one seeks to underscore the most positive aspects of Catholicism, one cannot be blind to the darker moments of the Catholic tradition. The Catholic Church has not been without corruption and authoritarianism. It has occasionally undermined the concept of individual responsibility, acted irrationally in the face of the advances of science, failed to rise to the challenges of the modern world, and fallen short of its own moral ideals. Church doctrine has not always been in harmony with reason, and although Christianity inspired the concept of equality, the Church has evolved very slowly in relation to gender equity. Many persons, even today, have suffered from these retrograde moments, and the Church has often been its own worst enemy. Fortunately, as a result of Vatican II, the Church has made an effort to acknowledge and learn from past shortcomings and failures. In defending the idea of a Catholic university, I seek to emphasize the highest dimensions of the Catholic tradition, those which have allowed the Church to criticize its own most deficient moments and those which can foster a great university.

Owing to the integration of certain ideal aspects of a rich Protestant and secular culture, with its elevation of autonomy and, with it, freedom of inquiry, Catholic universities in the United States have tended to avoid the darker sides of Catholicism. Recognition of the autonomy of the individual, which could be said to be a just extension of the basic Christian idea of the dignity of the human person, but which was fully articulated only in the wake of the Protestant break from Catholicism, has become a central part of most American Catholic universities. No university, Catholic or otherwise, that lacks such freedom is simultaneously respected as a great university. Not surprisingly, for the world's strongest Catholic universities one looks to the United States, where this ideal of academic freedom is present. Academic freedom is not just an anomaly that happens to be part of the American scene, it is the heart and soul of what makes American universities great. To allow for independent Catholic universities that can compete with the most outstanding non-Catholic universities in the world is in Catholicism's best interest. While it is certainly wise to sound an alarm when some

Catholic universities do not integrate into their mission statements or ideals the concept of Catholic character, the Church should not go so far as to destroy the conditions that have given rise to the world's most eminent Catholic universities. It need not play into the hands of those who might agree with Shaw's witticism.

Catholic universities in America have integrated the highest ideals of Protestantism not least of all because they seek to flourish in a highly competitive environment. An institution that measures itself against others is naturally encouraged to absorb and integrate the best ideas and strategies of the competition. A friendly rivalry forces an institution to bring to the fore the very best it has to offer, knowing that if it is deficient, others will supersede it. There is a significant difference between Catholic culture in those countries that are predominantly Catholic, such as the Mediterranean countries, and those countries, Germany and the United States, for example, where Catholicism competes with other faith traditions. Engagement with others encourages a Catholic culture, or a Catholic university, to reach its greatest potential and to learn from other models.

Because Catholic universities in the United States compete with Protestant and secular universities, they often assimilate their best aspects. Not only do Catholic universities integrate their ideas and strategies, they also seek out faculty members who are not Catholic but who feel very much at home at a religious university. As Protestant universities have divested themselves of their Christian heritage, the Catholic university has become one of the few places where religious scholarship can truly flourish alongside secular scholarship. Not surprisingly, then, Catholic universities have become increasingly attractive to religious intellectuals of all kinds, and some of the most distinguished professors and highest academic leaders at American Catholic universities are non-Catholics. The Vatican II decree on ecumenism, *Unitatis Redintegratio* (1964), gives a rationale for the participation of non-Catholic Christians in the intellectual life of a Catholic university. Also, the active presence of religious non-Christians can help a Catholic university realize a richer sense of the community of humanity and the mystery of God, a position underscored in the Vatican II decree on non-Christian religions, *Nostra Aetate* (1965).

The danger that has been sounded in recent debates, for example, by James Burtchaell, C.S.C., in *The Dying of the Light*, is that the Catholic university will become like the other, more dominant models: it will become more secular than Catholic.[2] The pull of mainstream culture is so powerful that not only does a minority institution integrate many of its features, in doing so, it risks relinquishing its own distinguishing traits. Such a development would not only hinder opportunities for a university to flourish as Catholic, it would restrict the diversity of

American higher education, which benefits from its religious and its nonreligious institutions, its liberal arts colleges and its research universities, its highly selective institutions and those with open admissions.[3] Obscuring a Catholic university's distinguishing marks would not be in anyone's best interest: no culture benefits from a monopoly of ideas. For this reason, I would like to reflect on the distinctive nature of the Catholic university in a setting that is enriched by Protestant and secular ideals. What, then, distinguishes the ideal Catholic university in this setting?

Spirituality in general and Catholicism in particular enrich the liberal arts experience, with its ideal of educating the whole person. At a Catholic university prayer and liturgy are a central part of the student's experience. Spiritual questions arise in all disciplines. Perhaps only in a religious setting, where reflection on God, or, metaphysically stated, the absolute, is prevalent do we address life's most fundamental questions, which are increasingly set aside at nonreligious institutions of higher learning.[4] Religion also brings to the liberal arts ideal a strong existential component. At a Catholic university students pursue theology not as the disinterested science of religious phenomena but as faith seeking understanding. They study history and the classics in order to learn not simply *about* the past, but also *from* the past. Students employ the quantitative tools of the social sciences not simply as a formal exercise with mathematical models but in order to develop sophisticated responses to pressing and complex social issues. In a world in which scholarship has often become antiquarian, disenchanted, and even cynical, at Catholic universities a connection to values and existential aspirations shapes intellectual inquiry. The generous commitment of sponsoring religious orders to Catholic campuses and the ways in which their members serve as role models reinforce this integration of education and character, of college and community, of faith and life. This spiritual dimension enriches the liberal arts ideal in ways that even the best liberal arts colleges can only approximate.[5]

A second obvious point is that at a Catholic university, religion is not separated from the curriculum or from scholarship but is fully integrated into both areas.[6] Faith is not an add-on to learning, restricted to residential life; it is integrated into the realm of inquiry, woven into each subject of study. Not only do students take required courses in theology and explore interdisciplinary programs of study that focus on religious subjects, such as Catholic social tradition, or religion and literature, but Catholic universities commonly define their research foci in the light of their Catholicism, recognizing the formal advantage of having a distinct niche and the substantive advantage of underscoring thereby their Catholic mission. Many Catholic universities, for example, have established premier programs in philosophy and theology as well as medieval studies. Some have strengths in various ethnic and geographic spheres where Catholicism is a dominant cultural marker, such as Latino studies, Irish studies, Polish studies, and Latin American studies. At a Catholic university religious and intellectual history, including the history of Christianity, is normally well represented. Also frequently privileged are classics and art history. Modern literature departments at Catholic universities may have unusual expertise in literature and religion, or literature and philosophy. Music departments may have several faculty members whose specialty is sacred music. Sociology may include among its emphases family, stratification, and religion. A department of economics may focus on problems facing humanity, such as development, health, and education. In departments of political science, comparative politics and political philosophy may be among the strongest areas; in addition, peace studies and the study of religion and politics are common subfields. A Catholic university's psychology department may stress developmental psychology and the related issues of poverty, family, and moral development, as well as fields that are central to a contemporary understanding of the human being, such as cognitive psychology. Among the strengths in science and engineering may be biomedical research, including diseases of developing countries, and environmental studies. A variety of areas of emphasis, of which these are simply examples, will reinforce one another on a given campus. Because most Catholic universities are small in relation to large state universities, they benefit when they develop foci for their departments and centers, ideally, ones that overlap with allied areas. Catholicism can provide a meaningful anchor for synergies of this kind.

If the Catholicism of Catholic universities were reduced, however, to enriching the liberal arts ideal with a spiritual dimension, these universities would not differ greatly from any number of Christian colleges. And if their Catholicism were reduced to the development of a distinct curricular and scholarly focus, Catholic universities would not differ, at least formally, from any number of other universities that have developed niche identities with overlapping spheres. The integration of spiritual and residential life and the rich orchestration of a broader scholarly identity may be significant dimensions of most Catholic universities, but these two dimensions, as important and unusual as they are, even in their combination, do not exhaust a university's Catholic identity. Indeed, it would be fair to say that they have more to do with religious identity than with Catholic identity per se. What, then, marks the Catholicism of a Catholic university?

My answer focuses on Catholicism's universalism (part I), its sacramental vision (part II), its elevation of tradition and reason (part III), and its emphasis on the unity of knowledge (part IV).

These four points could be loosely related to the different persons of the Trinity and the idea of the Trinity itself: the idea of one God grants dignity to all persons, regardless of their nation or background; the Incarnation, or the life of Christ, illuminates the idea of divine presence in the world; the Holy Spirit manifests itself in the development of the Catholic tradition, with its elevation of reason; and the Trinity itself underscores the organic connections between each of these spheres and the world, which is a manifestation of divine wisdom. As Christian as these four points might be, I present them as distinctive in relation to various strands of Protestantism and the modernist era they helped to generate, while at the same time recognizing that any great Catholic university will integrate the best of the Protestant and modern traditions, even as it remains distinct. In addition, any great Catholic university will speak to the most contemporary of our concerns, though it may do so not least of all because of its countercultural tendencies, which offer us insights that have all too often been forgotten or left undeveloped.

Beyond seeing in the person of Jesus Christ the embodiment of divine wisdom, the Catholic tradition also recognizes in the Incarnation a profound integration of metaphysics, ethics, and the philosophy of history, including the ideas that self-sacrifice on behalf of the universal is among the highest of human principles and that the good should be realized in this world. To search for broader conceptual terms in articulating our Christian vision to others is even more important today when one reflects on the increasing loss of faith among contemporary intellectuals and academics. Pope John Paul II writes in paragraph 104 of his encyclical *Fides et Ratio:* "Philosophical thought is often the only ground for understanding and dialogue with those who do not share our faith."

I

A defining aspect of Catholicism is the stress on universalist principles and, with this, an emphasis on community and love. The Reformation was a revolution of the autonomous subject, and although it was not without an extraordinary impact on Catholicism itself, Catholicism nonetheless elevates to an unusual degree the embeddedness of the individual within a collective identity. Catholic students, therefore, may find it fairly easy to identify with larger institutions and with tradition. This identification gives them an intuitive resistance to aspects of modernity, including the tendency toward excessive reflection on one's own particularity that may be said to characterize much of contemporary culture. In my own experience, students who enroll at Catholic universities tend to be not as preoccupied with their own identity, not as self-absorbed or as unsure of their place in the world, as are the students one encounters at secular institutions.

America has been fertile ground for the Protestant elevation of individuality. Indeed, individuality and autonomy are distinguishing dimensions of American culture, as the Bill of Rights so clearly demonstrates. Not only our country, but also our age, is attached to the concepts of subjectivity and particularity. In the postmodern rejection of universals, for example, we recognize this characteristic elevation of particularity. The Catholic student is likely to gain insight into the value of individuality and particularity simply by living in contemporary America. What Catholicism, with its emphasis on universals, offers in contradistinction to this culture has both supertemporal value on its own and contemporary relevance as a balance against the excesses of both our culture and our age.

Christianity recognizes only one God, before whom all persons are equal, irrespective of their origin. Out of the concept of a single God for all humankind and the idea that all human beings are in the image of God and thus "partakers of the divine nature" (2 Pet. 1:4), Christianity developed the concept of universal human rights, with its emphasis on the dignity of every individual and the value of the common good. This concept and its concomitant obligations toward other persons, especially the underprivileged and the underserved, are the inspiration behind the scholarly focus on social justice issues, including issues of poverty and development, that we find at Catholic universities, and it helps explain the Catholic emphasis, perhaps most pronounced at Vincentian universities, on educating immigrants and first-generation college students. While social justice issues may be most visible in the humanities and the social sciences, they also animate professional programs. A business program at a Catholic university seeks to educate knowledgeable professionals whose work is informed by moral principles. A college of engineering views its research as the utilization and development of the earth's resources in order to help humanity and thereby serve as an agent for God's work. A school of architecture views its mission as involving not only artistic self-expression but also service to the community.

Today, at least three issues with profound implications for coming generations deserve special consideration at a Catholic university. First, the general crisis of values and orientation, resulting from cultural changes and from complex developments in science, technology, the global economy, and world politics. Efforts to address this crisis must pervade the entire curriculum, from philosophical and theological ethics to the applied ethics of the professional schools. Second, the increasing gap between developed and developing countries, a topic of great concern to a universalist religion. Third, the ecological crisis and the related question of sustainable development or the ability to meet the needs of the present without compromising the ability of future generations to meet their needs. Addressing this crisis requires truly collaborative work, and it is intimately connected to both the crisis of values and the increasing tensions between developed and developing countries. All three of these issues—the ethical challenges of modernity, global economic and social justice, and the protection of nature—are addressed in the 1990 apostolic constitution on Catholic universities, *Ex Corde Ecclesiae*.

Personal identity is nourished by one's sense of community and one's connection to broader, universal values. A Catholic university's stress on community harkens back to the origins of the first universities in medieval Europe and the nineteenth-century origins of many of America's first Catholic universities, which involved intense interaction between faculty and students, who often lived and learned under one roof. Even today, students at Catholic universities are extraordinary in their attachment to their residential communities and colleges, especially when this sense of community has been strengthened by a vibrant liturgical life.[7] The Catholic mass is a celebration of communion, not only with Christ, but also with the other participants. When a crisis arises on a Catholic campus, students rally to support one another, as do faculty. A core set of curricular requirements often underscores this sense of community and companionship.[8] In this context, a Catholic university ideally elevates those disciplines that help students better grasp the richness of collective identity, including the arts, which contribute not only to an individual's search for edification, but also to the collective identity of a culture. If one of the distinguishing features of Protestantism is the elevation of the individual subject, and one of the factors in the dissolution of Protestant universities as religious institutions was the relegation of the religious dimension to the private sphere, as George Marsden has argued in *The Soul of the American University*, the Catholic tradition may be more resistant than its Protestant counterpart to this factor of secularization, for its elevation of collective identity and its integration of religion with the public sphere are far more pronounced.

Inspired by an idea of community that always extends toward a larger whole, Catholic universities offer a climate that encourages active participation in community service endeavors. On many campuses Catholic undergraduates eagerly pursue experiential learning and service opportunities, and a significant percentage of graduating seniors dedicate themselves to community service. One of the most competitive programs for graduating seniors across the United States is the Alliance for Catholic Education, which supplies teachers, working for a salary not much higher than the minimum wage, to more than eighty parochial schools in the urban and rural southern United States. Because calculating self-interest seems to be a more dominant characteristic of the age than self-transcendence, this devotion to the common good and to the poor and needy is unusual and impressive. Certainly, Catholic universities are not alone in pursuing moral education and community involvement. Many faculty members at non-denominational universities are models of caring who take great interest in the moral education of their students. Indeed, Catholic universities can learn from those secular universities that have already assumed leadership roles in these areas, especially in the integration of service learning and disciplinary expertise. What makes Catholic universities distinctive, however, is the explicit institutional commitment to these values, which tends to be less explicit and therefore increasingly less secure at secular universities. Whereas Catholic universities may suffer the danger of hypocrisy when they do not live up to their ideals, the danger at many secular universities is greater still: quietly abandoning ideals that once motivated almost every university in this country and simply preparing students for critical thinking, divorced from the moral realm, and for career preparation, independently of the concepts of character, citizenship, and vocation.

Whatever its historical origins or regional focus may be, a truly Catholic university is in its ultimate telos international. Internationalism is part of Catholicism's extraordinary attraction and mystique. The study of theology or philosophy, of art or psychology, is driven by questions and insights that transcend national and economic borders; in this sense the ideal university is international and open to students regardless of their financial resources. The international identity of a Catholic university may manifest itself in diverse ways, such as a high percentage of international students or of recent immigrants; the hiring of scholars from countries beyond the home country; a significant investment in foreign languages, literatures, and cultures; a high percentage of students studying abroad or pursuing opportunities for service in other countries; or the development of interdisciplinary institutes that address issues of transnational concern. The Catholic's moral responsibilities are not simply familial, local, or national, but extend to the international community and indeed to future generations.

II

A defining aspect of the modern secular world is the *verum-factum* principle, or the idea, first fully developed in the seventeenth century, that only what is constructed by humanity has truth and value.[9] This view has had extraordinary importance for the development of new knowledge in mathematics, for a model of science as experimentation, and for the modern era's confluence of science, technology, and capitalism. However, it has also led over time to diminishing respect for what is already given—God, nature, tradition, other selves, and an ideal sphere of meaning. Seeing all positions as human constructions, this perspective ultimately negates every objective order and, with it, any moment of higher meaning or transcendence. Contemporary culture studies rightly recognize that our views on moral and other issues have changed through time and that many positions taken to be supertemporally valid were in fact merely contingent. Many advocates of culture studies conclude from this development that all positions are constructed and that none are objectively valid. Recognition and validity, however, are not one and the same. Not all valid norms are recognized by every culture, as slavery, for example, makes evident. Moreover, one can unveil something as a mere construct only insofar as it is seen to deviate from reality, which is thus presupposed as having innate dignity and transcending mere construction. According to the constructivist view, our obligations to other human beings can be revised in the light of our developing preferences, for even our highest moral principles are invented, not discovered. In contrast to this paradigm, the Catholic tradition elevates a sacramental vision that finds God in and through the world; correspondingly, it upholds the innate dignity of every human being and argues for the binding nature of the moral law.

The idea of God as wholly other, which is prominent in the negative or dialectical theology of Protestant modernity, contrasts with the Catholic view of God's presence in reality. In the words of the great philosopher and cardinal Nicholas of Cusa, God is the non-other (*non aliud*); this commonality is the basis for our elevation of human dignity and equality. To conceive of God as not present in the world would be, paradoxically, to limit Him. Even among Catholic thinkers who rightly stress that the mystery of God is inexhaustible, there is greater recognition of the presence of God in the world and greater optimism about our ability to make discoveries about God. The Protestant churches, in contrast, tend to place extraordinary emphasis on humanity's fall from God, taking a more pronounced view of original sin and its damaging effects on the world and ourselves. Protestants tend to be skeptical of the view that through human inquiry we can approach knowledge of God. The Catholic position argues that divine truth, beauty, and goodness are reflected in this world and that the effects of original sin are not so severe as to prevent humans from knowing this reflection and, through such knowledge, coming closer to God. The Catholic tradition has evolved a model of reconciliation and forgiveness that offers hope for the salvation of all. God is so forthcoming in His love and forgiveness, so radiant in His illumination and mercy, that even the greatest sinners may be welcomed back into communion with God. Sacrament and community are here intertwined.

In stressing the presence of God in humanity and the ability of human reason to discern objective knowledge, the Catholic tradition seeks to celebrate both of the defining features of Christianity: the Incarnation, or God's entering the world as a human being, which gives rise to the sacramental vision of Catholicism; and the Trinity, including not only the concept of God as a relation or community, but also the idea that the Holy Spirit infuses this world with divinity in ways that extend beyond the singular appearance of Christ. This sacramental vision does not reduce divinity to thisworldliness. Catholicism points toward the transcendence that is contained in the world, thereby offering a counter-position to two mirroring elements of modernity: the secular tendency to see only immanence and no higher meaning in the world, and the Protestant tendency to project meaning beyond this world and so, by a different route, to divest this world of its higher meaning. The Catholic tradition seeks to recognize with the secular model the value of this world, and with the Protestant model the transcendence of divinity, which, though present in the world, is not exhausted by this world.

The Catholic position that recognizes divine presence in reality provides an alternative to the dominant secular view that every position is a construction and has therefore neither intrinsic value nor a claim on reality objectively stronger than any other. The Catholic intellectual sees the moral law as independent of human invention and as sacred. At the same time, it can be discovered via reason and is to be tested by argument; it need not be accepted simply on faith. The moral law includes certain absolute duties, which are not easy to follow, but which nonetheless give higher meaning to humanity. The idea that the moral law is fully rational and at the same time not alterable by humanity is markedly countercultural, but potentially very attractive in an age of disorientation. Certainly, the modernist project has broken away from two of the oldest, indeed ancient, aspects of religion, the delimiting of individual subjectivity and the sacredness of the moral law. It is, therefore, not surprising that a wider, nonreligious circle that is seeking orientation today may find something attractive at a Catholic university.

The Catholic idea that God is manifest in nature, and that nature has a certain intrinsic worth insofar as it is an instantiation of an ideal sphere, offers us a higher justification for the natural sciences. Biology, chemistry, and physics give us windows onto the divine structure of reality. The glory and truth of God are mirrored in creation. Indeed, the world is also a revelation, the *liber naturae*, which is to be studied along with the Bible or the *liber scripturae.* Further, the customs, institutions, and interaction of human beings have a hidden wisdom, which we are invited to explore through the social sciences. There are patterns in human history, and one of the historian's tasks is to discover the logic of historical development, the hidden order and reason behind the apparent randomness of history. Another obligation of the scholarly community is to ask in what ways our current world deviates from the ideal principles we ought to realize. The study of law at a Catholic university, for example, involves not only an introduction to the law and to legal practice but also a reflection on possible tensions between existing laws and principles of justice. The sacramental vision, which both elevates what is and measures what is against a higher ideal, gives greater dignity to the university enterprise than the current secular framework that reduces science and engineering to merely technical reason and reduces the social sciences, the humanities, and law to the merely contingent and the merely critical, severing in each case any connection to the transcendent.

The concept of sacramental vision also ennobles the arts. Art deals with the basic structures of being, nature, and spirit, spheres that are to be taken very seriously at a Catholic university. Indeed, art can be said to be higher than everyday reality insofar as it is closer to expressing truth: what we call everyday reality may have more aspects of deception, insofar as it shields us—by way of the capriciousness of situations and events, the clutter of external and superficial objects, and the immediacy of sensuous impressions—from a more essential meaning, a more genuine reality. The everyday world is not free of this higher spirit and essence, but art, unlike the everyday world, emphasizes and reveals this higher reality. In this sense art has a profound metaphysical dimension; it does not imitate the external world, rather, it makes visible for us the absolute and allows us to see the essences that superficiality sometimes covers. In addition, art can carry us to a position that is not simply a clearer sense of what is, but an inspiring and inspiriting sense of what should be. Art may render the ideal real. And when art shows what is less than ideal, it may offer a criticism of the negativity of reality, thus implying a higher ideal. The Catholic affirmation of the manifestation of God in the world underscores this elevation of art, whereas the Protestant traditions have often wrestled uncomfortably with any such attempt to render the absolute finite, to grasp the divine in the sensuous sphere. Of course art, like the sacraments themselves, not only gives us a window onto the transcendent, it leaves us with a sense of mystery and multivalence. Like the sacraments, great art is inexhaustibile.

In addition, art provides us with sacramental vision in a way that is extraordinarily open to diversity, a concept that has been rightly elevated in the last half century. Artistic masterpieces are possible of various kinds and from various traditions—

where one philosophical truth excludes competing truths, one sensuous representation does not exclude another. There are infinite ways of instantiating the ideal through beautiful expression. Therefore a variety of works can address a multiplicity of needs without limiting one another in an exclusive competition. Each age will seek newer, more diverse manifestations of beauty, which harmonize universal principles with the needs of the day. Art opens up for us the value of diversity and the richness of different stories, multiple traditions, and various vir-tues, even as we recognize through these works certain common aesthetic principles. One of the challenges of modern Catholicism is to integrate its universalism, which includes the concept of universal human rights, with recognition of the distinct contributions of indigenous cultures and the moments of other religious and cultural worldviews that can still enrich Catholicism as an emerging faith. It is here that Catholicism must continue to learn from modern secular culture, on the one hand, and world religions, on the other hand. But that is, of course, in the spirit of its own universalism.

III

Although in the United States Catholicism has frequently been viewed—and has viewed itself—as anti-intellectual, the Catholic tradition is on the whole a highly intellectual one. Indeed, a distinguishing feature of Roman Catholicism is its profound integration of Hellenic thought. Through the centuries Roman Catholicism has placed great emphasis on philosophical argument and historical tradition. Instead of basing its claims solely on the Scriptures, it has attended to the philosophical development of the Church, as guided by the Holy Spirit. This is another great difference between the Protestant and Catholic traditions. Not only do the Protestant traditions elevate the individual's private and unmediated relationship to God, many of them promote the Bible as the singular source of religious wisdom. The *sola scriptura* perspective is vastly different from the Catholic emphasis on reason and tradition.

The elevation of tradition and reason has various consequences. First, philosophy and theology have always played central roles in the Catholic Church. As a result, Catholic universities have tended to retain their requirements in philosophy and theology when most non-Catholic peer institutions have abandoned any privileging of these disciplines. Catholic thinkers acknowledge that there are deficiencies in focusing on the Bible's literal and historical meaning at the expense of its spiritual meaning, its broader significance and truth, including its coherence for the present. As a result, Catholics are less susceptible to the crisis that arises from the application of historical-critical methods in biblical criticism. An elevation of the Holy Spirit may free us from a crisis of faith when scholars in pursuit of historical details inform us that some of the most central elements of the Christian faith did not originate with Christ, but emerged in the wake of later reflections. The more one recognizes reason as the core of Christianity, the more one is comfortable abstracting from certain contingent moments.

The idea that faith and reason may function as a higher harmony was a common insight in the medieval culture of all three great monotheistic religions but is increasingly rare in modernity. The Catholic Church embraces this interconnection of faith and reason against the current of the times, as is evident in *Fides et Ratio*. The elevation of reason does not contradict faith. Grace and providence are transcendent forces that we neither control nor fully grasp. Prayer and faith open our eyes to positions not immediately accessible to reason, but which reason may eventually support once it is led down this path. One longs to know what is only partially understood via revelation. Moreover, even though true faith cannot contradict the rigorous use of reason, it can enrich our grasp of the mystery and inexhaustible potential of truth, of the inexplicable complexity of life and transcendence. In this way, however articulate one might be, however involved one's philosophical arguments might be, the moment of wonder does not disappear. Faith is no longer uncritical and unquestioning, but it remains as a moment of elegant simplicity and acceptance.

Second, the elevation of reason suggests that the Catholic intellectual is eager to learn from other traditions and new perspectives. Every position is to be entertained and weighed in the service of truth. This diminution of ourselves and this sense of the transcendent, our desire for new perspectives through reason, and, quite simply, the elevation of the value of all persons lead a Catholic university to welcome persons of diverse faiths. Such a university gladly embraces those who, with intelligence and respect, can challenge and complement the Catholic character of the institution. As part of a universal Church, the Catholic university must seek to cultivate the inspiring model of those medieval thinkers from the three great monotheistic religions who so elevated reason that they sought out competing traditions in order to see what was of value in them and to ask how these might relate to their own. A great Catholic university pursues alternative positions either to ensure that its own positions measure up to reason, or to adjust them accordingly. The Catholic university challenges its students in ways that require them to weigh the strengths and weaknesses of the Catholic tradition and to confront Catholic values with other religious values and with contemporary cultural values. It challenges them to weigh arguments for and against. Ideally, this dialogue involves not only our interlocutors in the

Jewish, Muslim, Protestant, and secular traditions, but also persons from other religious traditions across the world, including Hindus and Buddhists. Dialogue not only within the Catholic and wider Christian community but also with all religious people and indeed with the whole human community underlies Paul VI's first encyclical, *Ecclesiam Suam* (1964). Reason necessarily fosters universalism, and the common search for truth binds persons of different backgrounds and orientations.

Third, because of the great emphasis on tradition, the Catholic Church gives us a rich array of intellectual and artistic works to study. The history of art is inextricably linked with Catholicism: through the early modern period, the Church was the greatest patron of the arts, and virtually all art was created in the service of God. At a Catholic university one finds great respect for artistic traditions and for the wisdom of the ages, not only for the Christian tradition itself, but also for antiquity, which so profoundly shaped the early Church. Accordingly, the humanities tend to be especially strong at Catholic universities. In addition, the study of law at Catholic universities has drawn considerably on the natural law tradition in order to shed light on modern dilemmas. Insofar as the Catholic tradition offers us images and arguments that stand in contrast to the clichés of the present, it gives us a lens with which to defend—against the currents of the age—the study of the great transcendental values of truth, beauty, and goodness. The Catholic tradition offers us a range of viewpoints with which to analyze contemporary value questions and to criticize some of the fashionable dogmas of the age. Because of its emphasis on received wisdom and its relationship to the Catholic tradition and the mission of the Church, a Catholic university offers its faculty and students the advantage of being able to move more quickly and more frequently to deeper and more detailed levels of discussion, which is only possible if certain presuppositions are shared and not constantly revisited. The richness of the tradition and the Christian elevation of reason also give Catholic universities a certain confidence when confronting some of the anti-rational tendencies that have made their way into the inner chambers of many of America's best secular universities.

Fourth, the Catholic university cannot shy away from philosophy and science, as they lead us to unexpected insights. In the long run, truth prevails, and the Church need not fear the truth. As a Catholic university contemplates potential tensions between its aspirations as a research university and its goals as a Catholic institution, academic freedom is of great importance. American Catholic universities have consistently upheld academic freedom as a defining feature of the Catholic university, and this ultimately does not threaten the university's identity as Catholic. The defense of academic freedom need not arise only from the Protestant elevation of the autonomy of the individual; it can equally derive from the Catholic elevation of truth as that which is best discovered by our having listened carefully to all possible positions. Academic freedom is intertwined with responsibility to the truth; each presupposes the other. The Catholic Church benefits from sound internal criticism, and it gains when it can address the issues of the age in the most cogent ways. Not only does Catholicism enhance the research university, the research university benefits Catholicism. Even as faith guides reason, reason guides the development of the Church, which remains a dynamic and living institution. Although one is naturally humble before the wisdom of the centuries, reason does at times lead to the revision of tradition, which in many cases may simply mean the return to a richer (and underdeveloped) moment in the tradition itself. The Catholic does not simply receive the accumulated wisdom of tradition, she seeks with the full array of her intellectual capacities to work through tradition, recognizing the logic of its development and raising questions about those elements of contemporary doctrine that invite still greater critical reflection. One of the most important issues for a Catholic intellectual is to think through—in debate with others and with the Church—which moments of the Church have universal validity and which are merely historical and contingent. In moving from the reception of tradition to reflection on tradition, we strive to bring not only ourselves and the tradition, but also the absolute, to self-consciousness, for the Holy Spirit works through the community of the Church in its historical development. The Catholic Church offers not only a sacramental but also a mediating vision.

Reason must be allowed to enrich our sense of intellectual community in every way. Catholic students tend to be at ease with tradition, which makes them more stable, a potential virtue in a world of flux; being anchored in supertemporal values, they may be more resistant to the faddishness of the age; and being convinced of the broadly communal nature of humanity, they have an extraordinary sensibility to the poor and the underprivileged. This admirable sense of embeddedness also carries with it, however, a potential danger, toward which we must be vigilant. In their deference to tradition and authority, Catholic students must work to gain the autonomy and independence, the critical judgment, expected of a college graduate. Catholic students are sometimes described as timid, naive, modest, deferential. So at home within a framework of community and a set of givens, they are also at times not as ambitious or intellectually demanding of themselves as might be desirable. The modern concept of the "self-made" man, which is a social analogue of the *verum-factum* principle, is not without its appealing dimensions, and here Catholicism is at a modest disadvantage. Intellectual autonomy and a sense of achievement can be undervalued in a world that elevates tradition and community, and so it is not surprising that graduates of even the most highly ranked Catholic universities have tended to earn a more modest percentage of doctorates than have graduates of secular peer universities.[10] A Catholic university must encourage its students to become intellectually ambitious, to recognize not only the modern Christian ideal of active service to the community but also the more traditional Christian ideal of contemplation. In this spirit, a Catholic university should foster a student-centered learning environment that elevates discussion over lecture. In addition, it should make an effort to expose students to the complexities and debates within the very tradition with which they identify. A Catholic university must emphasize its students' obligations to develop themselves to the greatest extent, so that they may fully cultivate the gifts with which they have been endowed, including reason.

The Protestant elevation of subjectivity has led a considerable number of its theologians and believers to focus on God the Father or, more frequently, on Christ in such a way as almost to lose sight of the third person of the Trinity. A Catholic university that elevates community and reason is likely to devote greater attention to the Holy Spirit, which represents a more communal and fully intersubjective ideal. One of the riddles of the Trinity is that although the complete Trinity is immanent in God the Father—for example, in the immediate connection between *one* God and *all* persons being children of that God—only in the Holy Spirit is the full truth of the Trinity revealed. Christ's death not only reveals the extreme humanity of God and Christ's willingness to pay for truth with His own life, it also frees divinity from particularity and releases it for the universal community of humanity, for which Christ sacrificed Himself. The love and salvation of Christ inspire, and reconstitute themselves in, the communal love of humanity: the truth of Easter is Pentecost. This pneumatic view of Christianity is appropriate for a Catholic university that elevates love and truth and recognizes that the Holy Spirit fulfills itself in those institutions that foster community, reason, and transcendence in communion with the Church.

IV

Unlike earlier eras in which a single value provided an overarching framework for the different spheres of life, as did God in the Middle Ages, the modern, secular world is characterized by a splintering of the spheres of life into autonomous subsystems, each of which has its own inner logic: this disintegration of values is reflected in such phrases as "l'art pour l'art" and "business is business" as well as in the separation of politics and morality, law and justice, or sexuality and love. Modern culture tends to view the diverse subsystems of modern life—from science to art—as autonomous and beyond moral judgment. Similarly, the modern value-free university, not just value-free in its application of the techniques of the social sciences but value-free in its ultimate purpose, consists of an array of parallel and unintegrated spheres. In the past centuries and increasingly in the past decades, new disciplines have emerged that have led to greater and greater precision of inquiry, but often at the cost of their contribution to a broader sphere. Because the modern self does not view itself as embedded in the cosmos and because the faculty member does not often see herself contributing beyond her subspecialty, her own endeavors are often divested of the dignity of contributing to a higher purpose. The modern secular university has become "an intellectual department store" (Jaspers 88), a "multiversity" (Kerr 1), where disciplines develop side by side and scholars pursue independent pursuits with no sense of connection or overarching purpose.

The Catholic tradition, inspired by the concept of the unity of knowledge, seeks in contrast to cultivate meaningful and integrative thought across the disciplines and argues that morality is not one sphere separate from the others but that it infuses all spheres: one can and should ask moral questions of architecture, art, business, engineering, law, politics, science, society, even religion. What is, should be measured against a transcendent and overarching set of norms, and the diverse spheres of inquiry should be studied to illuminate one another. The Catholic Church, in its universalism, has preserved and enriched the classical concept that truth is ultimately one, that the diverse branches of human knowledge can be integrated and synthesized, and that a greater harmony exists among the spheres of knowledge, which are complexly interwoven and interrelated. This stress on unity is rare in an age in which the specialist does not often ask the broader questions about the relation of particular knowledge to the organic structure of knowledge or about the greatness and limits of her own disciplinary contributions. Indeed, philosophy, whose task has traditionally been to pursue such questions, has itself all too often become simply another subdiscipline pursuing its own particular knowledge.[11]

In its ideal sense, philosophy, which has a privileged role at Catholic universities, attends to the whole and to the basic principles of the individual sciences. In an era of exponentially increasing knowledge, this task has become ever more demanding, but this difficulty does not diminish the regulative idea. Philosophy must continue to concern itself with connections among the disciplines and ask larger questions, including normative questions, with one eye directed toward the answers given by earlier generations and another eye attentive to the moral dilemmas and responses of the contemporary age. Whereas contemporary American philosophy has become increasingly specialized and removed from the historical tradition, theology has provided a welcome counterweight, retaining a rich relationship to tradition and pursuing questions that still concern students today. Similarly, the best philosophy programs at Catholic universities have sought to integrate the technical expertise of analytic philosophy with historical knowledge and the continuing cultivation of broader questions.

The Catholic elevation of philosophy and theology enriches not only the moral focus but also the holism of a university education. When faculty members at a Catholic university discuss poverty in the classroom, they address it with attention to several overlapping fields: its theological and philosophical implications; its articulation in literature and the arts; and its psychological, economic, political, and sociological aspects. The ideal of philosophy as the discipline that seeks connections across disciplines provides us with a model of inquiry that is necessary if we are to solve the many objective problems of the age, which, because of the increasing complexity of the contemporary world, require approaches that unite the diverse disciplines. The modern research university must be interdisciplinary if it is to have any hope of tackling the pressing issues of the day. I name as one example among many the ecological problem. Collaborative work across the disciplines is a moral imperative. Any such integration should draw on the reflections of not only individual researchers working in their disciplines, but also philosophers and theologians who seek to integrate advances in these disciplines within a systematic frame. At the same time, we must avoid the dangers of any system that operates without regard for the emergence of new knowledge or that shies away from the necessary revision of systematic claims previously thought to be final. Integration, like the unfolding of the Holy Spirit in history, is always a work in progress.

Because of their consistent elevation of service and community, on the one hand, and reason and inquiry, on the other hand, most Catholic universities combine teaching and research in their mission statements. The integration of both teaching and research places a Catholic university in a privileged position to explore the unity of knowledge across disciplines. Catholic universities should hire faculty members who have a passionate commitment to their discipline and a love of teaching. Such scholars tend to do research in the very areas they teach; not often overly specialized, they are interested in communicating their thoughts to a wider audience, including undergraduates with diverse majors. Having as teachers researchers who can bring to the classroom not only an interest in other subjects but the most recent knowledge in their fields, and the critical skills and passions of active researchers, is ideal for students. Not only does research enhance teaching, teaching aids research. The engagement with students forces faculty members to think of the most basic principles of their fields, and seminar experiences where discussion is rich and vital can lead at all levels to the production of new knowledge. No less important, teaching forces faculty members to communicate clearly. Indeed, accessible writing can be viewed as a form of teaching, and the greatest teachers are often the clearest writers. In addition, the teacher who is also a researcher has had her ideas tested by a broader audience. While seclusion and quiet may be presuppositions for the formulation of new knowledge, its genesis often presupposes dialogue, and its reception and full analysis necessarily presuppose dialogue.

Bridging the liberal arts college and the research university, America's leading Catholic universities are the ideal size for interdepartmental dialogue—with enough scholars to form clusters of strength but not so many that faculty members cannot seek out intellectual partners in conversation from other departments. Aristotle suggests in the *Politics* that there is a quantitative limit to the *polis* (1326a–b). This could be said of the university as well, and many research universities challenge this limit, effectively discouraging dialogue across the disciplines and elevating by default overspecialization, which is one of the greatest dangers to contemporary intellectual inquiry. Certainly, new insights arise more readily among specialists, but the value of these new insights is lost if the researcher is not able to place them within the broader landscape of intellectual inquiry. To satisfy this more ambitious goal, we need breadth of knowledge, clarity of expression, and a culture of dialogue. A Catholic university is well-positioned to satisfy these expectations. It can do so partly because of its attachment to the Catholic ideal of integrating thought across disciplines and communicating it to the larger community. Whereas many contemporary universities now call for interdisciplinary curricula, most Catholic universities have long sought both interdisciplinary and integrative knowledge. This is manifest in a variety of ways, from university mission statements and the organization of curricula to the development of interdisciplinary institutes and the goal of hiring broad-ranging scholars. At a Catholic university one tends to find fewer scholars who overestimate the value of their specialized contributions, not recognizing that their work is but one small piece of a larger mosaic, and fewer researchers who secretly despair that their research could not animate anyone but another specialist in the same subdiscipline.

Not only teaching and research, but the liberal arts and the professional schools tend to be united at Catholic universities. The Catholic university addresses fundamental and normative questions and educates students in the liberal arts. At the same time, most Catholic universities offer students opportunities for applied knowledge in professional programs, such as architecture, business, education, engineering, or law. The presence of a liberal arts curriculum guarantees that students pursuing a practical degree or a preprofessional program also receive a broader education, and it ensures that foundational and normative questions are not ignored in the teaching and research of those in applied areas. The question of the higher rationale of specialized and applied disciplines is vigorously pursued, not avoided. Catholic universities enrich the liberal arts ideal by insisting that practical knowledge, like particular knowledge, though sought and cultivated, is nonetheless not exhaustive and is to be sublated into a knowledge, more philosophical in kind, that unites the diverse disciplines and rises toward a higher ideal of organic unity. The liberal arts curriculum helps students develop overarching intellectual virtues, such as being able to analyze a complex problem, formulate clear questions, and prepare a cogent argument. Guided by such a curriculum and by teachers who are themselves active scholars, students learn how to continue to learn in a changing world. Fortunately, the intellectual virtues that our students learn are not only their own reward and integral to the life of the mind, they are essential to any successful enterprise. The presence of the more practical disciplines keeps the Catholic university focused not only on issues of intrinsic value but also on questions of wider applicability.

Adding to this practical dimension is the passion for making a difference that manifests itself in students' devotion to community service. Historically, the integration of professional schools into Catholic universities provided a ladder for the development of generations of immigrants, who gained a vocation through which they could both improve themselves and help others, even as their minds were enriched by liberal learning and their souls enlivened by a Catholic community.[12]

The ideal of integrative knowledge seems foreign to modern consciousness, yet fragmentation and disjointedness are hardly defensible as ideals in themselves. The lost ideal of holistic knowledge provides, precisely in its foreignness, a valuable antidote to some of the weaknesses of the modern age and of the contemporary university. Not only does familiarity with a contrasting ideal offer the formal advantage of fostering critical distance toward the reigning ideals of one's own era, in this case the holistic model presents us with a substantive alternative, an ideal toward which a Catholic university is obliged to strive. This ideal can help address a broader crisis in higher education and in contemporary culture, a crisis that calls out for alternative models. Just as Catholic universities have benefited from integrating the best practices of secular universities, so the Catholic model of a university can enrich and enliven other universities, as they seek to fulfill their own highest aspirations.[13]

NOTES

This essay appeared in an earlier and different form in *The Future of Religious Colleges*, edited by Paul J. Dovre. Grand Rapids, Mich.: Eerdmans, 2002. 163-184.

1. Substantial and diverse attempts to articulate the distinctive nature of Catholic higher education can be found in the volumes edited by Gallin and Hesburgh. For a detailed account of the strengths and weaknesses of the most recent publication on the topic, O'Brien's *The Idea of a Catholic University*, see my forthcoming review in the *Journal of Higher Education*. The extraordinary obstacles to creating a great Catholic university in the secular era and the uneasiness many persons feel about articulating the Catholic character of such a university suggest that the topic demands continuing reflection and articulation. In *Negotiating Identity* Gallin notes this lack of articulation as one of the reasons for recent conflicts over the juridical application of the apostolic constitution *Ex Corde Ecclesiae*: "Although the presidents have reacted strongly against any proposal for a clear juridical relationship with the hierarchy, they have not been able to articulate with precision the characteristics of their institutions which they regard as giving it its Catholic identity" (182).

In trying to develop the idea of a Catholic university in language that transcends the Catholic tradition and may appeal to others, I have focused primarily on the intellectual aspects of Catholicism as they help to illuminate the mission of a Catholic university. I have not addressed topics in three related areas, each of which is equally deserving of extended treatment on its own. First, the richness of religion in general and of the Catholic tradition in particular could be explored in ways that transcend the *intellectual* appeal of Catholicism; religion is not reducible to intellectual concerns and cannot be exhausted by a philosophical perspective, even if it complements philosophy in countless ways. Second, the many ways in which a Catholic university functions as a university could be explored independently of its aspirations as a *Catholic* university, for example, its standards for promotion and tenure, its strategies for evaluating teaching, or its distribution of resources. Third, reflections on the specific institutional strategies one must employ to ensure that the Catholic ideal is realized in the university setting could be developed; such reflections would need to address, for example, faculty hiring, curricular development, and the full integration of academic and residential life. Advancement in these areas presupposes, however, the articulation of an ideal that can inspire the confidence and imagination of a university community.

2. A contrasting and more optimistic view of the future of religious higher education can be found in Benne.

3. Great diversity exists even among religious and Christian institutions of higher learning, as is demonstrated in Hughes and Adrian. Also, the missions of Catholic universities are various, often influenced by the particular history and orientation of the sponsoring religious order. As a result, my essay addresses an ideal type, which individual Catholic universities may reflect to varying degrees.

4. The failure of secular universities to engage the most ultimate questions about reality, including those that transcend the paradigm of disinterested science, is at the heart of O'Brien's critique of the secular university and his elevation of the idea of a Catholic university.

5. I differ here from John Henry Cardinal Newman in his classic study, *The Idea of a University*. In addition to the fact that I address some themes which he overlooks, partly because his focus is not solely on the idea of a *Catholic* university, our positions differ in three respects. First, in contrast to Newman, I view the university as a setting where knowledge and virtue ideally overlap, where moral formation is part of the college experience, and where the virtues of character are fostered as much as are the virtues of intellect. Second, whereas Newman sees teaching as the primary purpose of the university, I see teaching and research as equally valuable and mutually enriching endeavors. Third, whereas he sees the university as a setting for only liberal learning, I propose the value of an integration of liberal and practical learning. At the same time I fully embrace what I consider to be Newman's two overarching points: his defense of the value of liberal learning as an end in itself, and his elevation of the unity of knowledge. Paradoxically, precisely my endorsement of the unity of knowledge leads to my disagreements with his focus solely on teaching at the expense of research and on liberal learning at the expense of practical education.

In subsequent years Newman articulated a richer picture of the university. In his later and less known *Rise and Progress of Universities*, Newman argues for the value of not only intellectual discipline but also moral and religious formation (e.g., 49, 182, 228–229). His eventual recognition of the value of research is evident in his programmatic inauguration of *The Atlantis: A Register of Literature and Science*, designed specifically for the advancement and communication of research (see Newman's *My Campaign in Ireland*, esp. 430 and 433).

6. In his fine reexamination, Pelikan echoes Newman's concern with the separation of religion from the university curriculum. He laments that many universities across the world today ignore the religious sphere and so offer students a reduced form of knowledge (39–40).

7. For an account of residentiality at one Catholic university, see Malloy 135–153.

8. In the College of Arts and Letters at the University of Notre Dame, for example, the core curriculum consists of two courses in philosophy and two courses in theology; foreign language study equivalent to three semesters; three courses in the combined areas of history and social science, with at least one course in each area; two courses in mathematics and two courses in science; individual courses in the fine arts, in literature, and in writing; and a year-long seminar that explores by way of classical and contemporary works the topics of God, nature, self, and society.

9. The *verum-factum* principle was first recognized and articulated by Giambattista Vico in *De nostri temporis studiorum ratione* (sec. 4), *De antiquissima Italorum sapientia* (Book I, sec. 1), and *Scienza nuova* (para. 331).

It derives from the expressions "'verum' et 'factum' [. . .] convertuntur," or, truth and artifice are interchangeable (convertible), and "verum esse ipsum factum," or, what is true is what is made.

10. On average, in the 1980s 4.11% of Notre Dame undergraduates earned Ph.D.'s. At Georgetown and Boston College the figures were even lower, 3.86% and 2.80%, respectively; for comparison, consider Princeton at 12.22%, Rice at 9.22%, Duke at 7.05%, Northwestern at 5.89%, and Vanderbilt at 4.64%.

11. One of the world's leading Catholic philosophers, Alasdair MacIntyre, recognizes that when philosophy is reduced to the status of one more specialized discipline and no longer provides integration or seeks a unified, if complex, understanding of the order of things, it must lose its privileged place in the curriculum. In contrast to this now dominant practice, MacIntyre argues for a model of inquiry in which specialized knowledge is always related to a larger whole (5–9).

12. For the richest history of American Catholic higher education, see Gleason.

13. For helpful comments on this essay I am grateful to Neil Delaney, Bernd Goebel, Fran Hagopian, Nathan Hatch, Vittorio Hösle, Rev. John Jenkins, C.S.C., Rev. Edward A. Malloy, C.S.C., and Vincent McCarthy.

I would also like to thank Rev. Theodore M. Hesburgh, C.S.C., for his gracious support of this publication and his generous foreword.

WORKS CITED

"An Analysis of Notre Dame Undergraduates Going on for Doctorates," Institutional Research Report 98–08H. 1 June 2002. <http://www.nd.edu/~instres/home2/highlights.html>.

Benne, Robert. *Quality with Soul: How Six Premier Colleges and Universities Keep Faith with Their Religious Traditions*. Grand Rapids, Mich.: Eerdmans, 2001.

Burtchaell, James Tunstead, C.S.C. *The Dying of the Light: The Disengagement of Colleges and Universities from Their Christian Churches*. Grand Rapids, Mich.: Eerdmans, 1998.

Carter, Stephen L. *The Culture of Disbelief: How American Law and Politics Trivialize Religious Devotion*. New York: Basic Books, 1993.

Gallin, Alice, O.S.U. *Negotiating Identity: Catholic Higher Education since 1960*. Notre Dame, Ind.: U of Notre Dame P, 2000.

Gallin, Alice, O.S.U., ed. *American Catholic Higher Education: Essential Documents, 1967–1990*. Notre Dame, Ind.: U of Notre Dame P, 1992.

Gleason, Philip. *Contending with Modernity: Catholic Higher Education in the Twentieth Century*. New York: Oxford UP, 1995.

Hesburgh, Theodore M., C.S.C., ed. *The Challenge and Promise of a Catholic University*. Notre Dame, Ind.: U of Notre Dame P, 1994.

Hughes, Richard T., and William B. Adrian, eds. *Models for Christian Higher Education: Strategies for Success in the Twenty-First Century*. Grand Rapids, Mich.: Eerdmans, 1997.

Jaspers, Karl. *The Idea of the University*. Ed. Karl Deutsch. Trans. H. A. T. Reiche and H. F. Vanderschmidt. Boston: Beacon, 1959.

John Paul II. *Fides et Ratio: On the Relationship between Faith and Reason*. Boston: Pauline, 1998.

Kerr, Clark. *The Uses of the University*. 4th ed. Cambridge: Harvard UP, 1995.

MacIntyre, Alasdair. "Catholic Universities: Dangers, Hopes, Choices." *Higher Learning and Catholic Traditions*. Ed. Robert E. Sullivan. Notre Dame, Ind.: U of Notre Dame P, 2001. 1–21.

Malloy, Rev. Edward A., C.S.C. *Monk's Reflections: A View from the Dome*. Kansas City: Andrews McMeel, 1999.

Marsden, George. *The Soul of the American University: From Protestant Establishment to Established Nonbelief*. New York: Oxford UP, 1994.

Newman, John Henry Cardinal. *The Idea of a University Defined and Illustrated In Nine Discourses Delivered to the Catholics of Dublin In Occasional Lectures and Essays Addressed to Members of the Catholic University*. Ed. Martin J. Svaglic. Notre Dame, Ind.: U of Notre Dame P, 1982.

———. *My Campaign in Ireland. Catholic University Reports and Other Papers*. Aberdeen: King, 1896.

———. *Rise and Progress of Universities and Benedictine Essays*. Ed. Mary Katherine Tillman. Notre Dame, Ind.: U of Notre Dame P, 1982.

O'Brien, George Dennis. *The Idea of a Catholic Univer-sity*. Chicago: U of Chicago P, 2002.

Pelikan, Jaroslav. *The Idea of the University: A Reexami-nation*. New Haven: Yale UP, 1992.

Shaw, George Bernard. "The Author's Apology" to *Mrs Warren's Profession*. *Collected Plays with their Pref-aces*. New York: Dodd, 1975. 1:233-266.

Vico, Giambattista. *Opere*. 8 volumes in 11. Bari: Laterza & Figli, 1911–42.